CONTENTS

Introducing Wiltshire Mysteries

Six writers probe mysterious facets of Wiltshire.

Author, broadcaster and journalist David Foot sets the scene by writing about the essential mystery of the 'bulging treasure chest' that is Wiltshire, 'where mysteries multiply by the page.'

His fellow authors all show that Wiltshire 'creaks, groans and intrigues with its inexhaustible reserves of history.' David Mudd explores the county's greatest mystery, Stonehenge. Peter Underwood, President of the Ghost Club, investigates some Wiltshire hauntings. Polly Lloyd delves into local legend and folklore. Noel Welch visits Avebury, and Alison Poole looks at the phenomenon of strange circles in cornfields.

Words, photographs and drawings all combine to reveal especially commissioned chapters '. . . full of question marks. We are invited to finish reading and then to start pondering.'

This, Bossiney's first Wiltshire title, is a must for all who love this historic county – and especially those of us who enjoy the curious thrill of mystery.

The Old Bell at Malmesbury.

4

About the author
DAVID FOOT

David Foot writes regularly on cricket, soccer and rugby for various newspapers, including 'The Guardian' and 'The Sunday Express'. He has worked in radio and television and is the author of several books. His 'Harold Gimblett, Tormented Genius of Cricket' is rated one of the finest books of its kind. 'There has never been a cricket book quite like this,' wrote John Arlott. 'David Foot has written it with compassion, something not too far from passion, and sympathy. It is a remarkable achievement . . .' In 1984, David Foot wrote the Introduction to 'Strange Somerset Stories' and contributed a chapter entitled 'Midnight Poachers at East Coker'.

David Foot

Wiltshire Mysteries
by David Foot

WILTSHIRE to me means white horses – and black dogs. The horses dominate the downs and hillsides, the dogs the imagination.

Like no other county, Wiltshire creaks, groans and intrigues with its inexhaustible reserves of history. Every hamlet has a story to tell. Every country house supposedly has its ghost. Every hillock has its scars, real or imagined, from a distant battle.

We shall come back to the white horses and the black hounds later. We shall leave others in this book to probe and ponder perhaps Wiltshire's greatest mysteries of all: Avebury, Stonehenge and Silbury Hill. It is unlikely that they will come up with too many unchallengeable conclusions. Historians and successive generations of academics have tried too often and failed. These magnificent ancient monuments of ritual must simply take their place with all the county's other imponderables.

During the Sixties I worked in the television and radio newsroom of the BBC in Bristol. We received a great number of stories from the Warminster area. It was the era of UFOs. Arthur Shuttlewood, himself a professional journalist, became understandably pre-occupied with the subject. He wasn't alone, of course. Reports of sightings came in by the day. It was a marvellous outlet for fertile imaginations. Eccentrics queued, it seemed, to get on the 'phone and tell us all about it.

But some of the reports demanded an ear. They came from

'Every hamlet has a story to tell' and no doubt Castle Combe, that most perfect of English villages, has a tale or two to tell.

reasonable people. They gave graphic accounts of what they claimed they had seen. Others went out on nightly patrols, with their notebooks and their cameras. We were told of visitors from another planet; a few of our informants, unbridled in their enthusiasm – and, no doubt, imaginations – claimed actually to have made contact. The photographic evidence wasn't particularly impressive. Nor were the more outrageous stories. A hard core of believers remained unwavering in their convictions. Scientists and cranks came to Warminster to see for themselves. Some went away shaking their heads. Not all.

The cynics, and that included most of the media as far as I could see, eventually decided the sightings were getting out of hand. 'Don't forget the military are stationed in the area. Experiments are probably going on all the time.' It seemed a realistic explanation. We haven't heard so much about Unidentified Flying Objects zooming around Wiltshire's chalky downs for a number of years, although there has been a resurgence of interest with the mysterious circles which have appeared in cornfields in the county.

Wiltshire is one of my favourite counties. I am enthralled by the sheer physical contrasts – the folding hills that often appear bereft of habitation, the cosy, meandering river valleys, the woodlands with their enchanting russet shades of autumn. I see the sheep and think of the old wool factories. I see the racehorses in training and hear the distant crescendo of a Newmarket crowd. I see dream villages like Castle Combe or the National Trust's Laycock – and bask in an idyllic heritage.

Who can motor on like a philistine when there is the fifteenth century Porch House at Potterne to be seen? Or the Elizabethan Corsham Court? Or Capability Brown's Bowood – or evocative manors like Great Chalfield and Sheldon? I won't start talking of Wilton House, Stourhead or the majesty of Salisbury Cathedral itself. This isn't intended in any sense to be a travelogue.

Rather it is intended to whet the appetite for those who relish the

One of the seven white horses which were etched into Wiltshire's chalky downs by unknown hands.

The fifteenth century Porch House at Potterne.

by-ways, mental and literal, of mystery. Every district of Britain is shaped and fashioned by its history. This is reflected, when we come to Wiltshire, by the volume of superstition and legend that still persits. Country people pretend they are sophisticated and have long outlived the favourite tales of their particular village. But they haven't – and that is a considerable part of their charm.

You don't have to wander far from the centre of Devizes to find yourself tingling with a feeling of intrigue. There it is on the market

The market cross at Devizes, scene of an eighteenth century drama.

THE MAYOR AND CORPORATION OF DEVIZES
AVAIL THEMSELVES OF THE STABILITY OF THIS
BUILDING TO TRANSMIT TO FUTURE TIMES THE
RECORD OF AN AWFUL EVENT WHICH OCCURRED
IN THIS MARKET PLACE, IN THE YEAR 1753,
HOPING THAT SUCH RECORD MAY SERVE AS
A SALUTARY WARNING AGAINST THE DANGER
OF IMPIOUSLY INVOKING DIVINE VENGEANCE
OR OF CALLING ON THE HOLY NAME OF GOD
TO CONCEAL THE DEVICES OF FALSEHOOD
AND FRAUD.

ON THURSDAY THE 25TH OF JANUARY 1753
RUTH PIERCE OF POTTERNE IN THIS COUNTY,
AGREED WITH THREE OTHER WOMEN TO BUY
A SACK OF WHEAT IN THE MARKET EACH PAYING
HER DUE PROPORTION TOWARDS THE SAME:
ONE OF THESE WOMEN IN COLLECTING THE
SEVERAL QUOTAS OF MONEY, DISCOVERED A
DEFICIENCY, AND DEMANDED OF RUTH PIERCE
THE SUM WHICH WAS WANTING TO MAKE GOOD
THE AMOUNT: RUTH PIERCE PROTESTED THAT
SHE HAD PAID HER SHARE AND SAID SHE WISHED
SHE MIGHT DROP DOWN DEAD IF SHE HAD NOT.
SHE RASHLY REPEATED THIS AWFUL WISH: WHEN
TO THE CONSTERNATION AND TERROR OF THE
SURROUNDING MULTITUDE, SHE INSTANTLY
FELL DOWN AND EXPIRED, HAVING THE MONEY
CONCEALED IN HER HAND.

Capability Brown's Bowood, one of Wiltshire's magnificent houses.

cross: an inscription telling us pretty succinctly what happened to the hapless Ruth Pierce in the mid eighteenth century. Her crime? She cheated at the local market.

Many of the villages had their own witch. Ancient parishioners still pretend they knew her, though the stories were passed down by their own parents. Lydia Shears was one such witch. She liked her snuff and was seldom without her clay pipe. Her oddball home at Winterslow remained her private domain. She was renowned for her rural wisdom and country lore. She told the villagers how to treat their warts and their boils.

But because she was dirty and weird, the rumours built up about her. Some said she had dangerous powers. They kept their children far away from her. They blamed her for illness in the local community. Witches often had to live with fearful bigotry. Old Lydia, hardly an endearing woman but perhaps without malice, died

A dire warning to potential cheats. The Mayor and Corporation of Devizes took a tough line in 1753, they weren't going to have 'awful' events happening in their town. They put up this no-nonsense inscription on the market cross recalling the fraudulent dealings of Ruth Pierce.

15

'Who can motor on like a philistine when there is the Elizabethan Corsham Court to be seen'.

mysteriously. No-one was ever too sure of the cause of death. She suffered from the prevailing climate of superstition and innuendo.

It was well known, of course, that some of the Wiltshire witches boasted of their supernatural skills. They traded on their facility for 'witchcraft' and there were always murky hints about the black arts. Many churches sealed the fonts so that the witches couldn't get into the building and make off with consecrated water.

Certainly the county had a higher than usual proportion of witches. Some were quite innocuous. Their behaviour may have been eccentric but they had basically compassionate natures and were more ready to offer advice on how to terminate an unwanted pregnancy than to cast a spell. Old men of Wiltshire will still tell you, however, of the tales they heard as boys: of witches who untethered horses and rode with them back to their covens.

The hare has always been a metaphor for disquieting legend. Long ago I met an old woman from the country who refused steadfastly to eat hare. It wasn't the taste she objected to – more the connotations.

Ralph Whitlock, that marvellous writer of the wide canvas of country life in Wiltshire, used for years to contribute a column to the Western Gazette, the weekly paper where I began my journalistic life. His were the words I read first every Friday morning. I envied his knowledge; the people he described – simple rural dwellers – always appeared to me to have so much more grasp of the purpose of life than the politicians and statesmen.

Mr Whitlock would, from time to time, touch on the legends and superstitions of these country folk. He once described a particular custom, maybe peculiar to Wiltshire – I can't remember – intended as a rough, effective form of justice for philandering husbands or adulterous wives. The rest of the village would assemble, armed with tin cans and other domestic implements or drums, guaranteed to make an appalling noise. Then they'd march to the home of the miscreant and begin their unrelenting din. As a variation, they would hurl slops at the house. I suppose it was their way of saying: 'You'd better not try that again!'

We now come back to the white horses and the black dogs. 'Cottage' publisher Michael Williams, the man behind Bossiney Books, will admit his weakness for *strange stories*. He shares our fascination for legend, myth and the incomprehensible. There are many things he implies with his succession of titles on the theme, for which there will never be simple, human explanation. He invites us only to contemplate the wonderment of timeless history – and to tremble just a little at some of the manifestations.

This is Mr Williams' first steps into Wiltshire as a publisher. He is a sportsman at heart – never more so than when it comes to his beloved county cricket in Gloucestershire – and could it be that he is now partially seduced by Wiltshire's virtually unrivalled equestrian tradition? He once marvelled aloud to me about 'the mystery and magic of racehorses, the curious, complicated process of turning a handsome colt into a celebrated classic winner.'

The county has bred and trained magnificent racehorses for many years. There is nothing more pulsating than the thudding of hooves

17

Fred Darling, the Master of Beckhampton trained no fewer than nineteen classic winners. With him are jockey Gordon Richards and racehorse owner Lord Dewar.

across the Downs on a crisp morning soon after dawn. Mr Williams reminded me that Fred Darling, the Master of Beckhampton, trained no fewer than nineteen classic winners. Not too many of them were greys, of course, but the hillsides of Wiltshire abound with white horses, cut into the chalk as dramatic metaphors.

'There is nothing more pulsating than the thudding of hooves across the Downs.'

There are seven white horses – at Marlborough and Pewsey, Alton Barnes and Broad Hinton, Broad Town and Cherhill. And the most famous is at Bratton Down on the outskirts of Westbury. It was fashioned on the site of a previous horse, said, with suspect accuracy, to have been cut to commemorate King Alfred's victory over the Danes. There's a great fashion in the county for carving into the chalky turf; impressive replicas of regimental badges, denoting stays in Wiltshire during the two world wars, can also be seen.

But this is essentially a book about mystery, and horses are an inevitable part of the scenario. They are highly sensitive creatures.

Their ears prick at sounds and vibrations of which we aren't even aware.

In my mildly morbid teenage years I went through a phase of collecting epitaphs in the Westcountry. Tomb-stones, I discovered, titillated our curiosity with dozens of half-told stories. Maybe in deference to the consecrated ground on which the stone was placed, relatives felt duty-bound to wrap their colourful messages in discretion. Could there be anything more eerie than the words carved in the stone to commemorate the unusual death of village labourer, John Hill.

> *He was in a wagon laden with stone for building the parish church when one of the horses suddenly ran away. The wagon was upset and the stones fell upon him to kill him instantly. May all carters who read this take warning and never get in their wagons . . .*

What caused the horse suddenly to bolt? Was it, ignorant and superstitious village people were asking each other in hushed tones, the work of the devil when all poor John Hill wanted to do was beautify a place of orthodox worship? I am only sorry that I don't know which parish in the Westcountry contains the disquieting tombstones. It was either Somerset or Wiltshire.

In another Westcountry churchyard is this equally intriguing epitaph:

> *It was through a horse I lost my breath*
> *And cruel hands which caused my death*

If only we had been told more about this 1808 tragedy.

I move on from the horses to the dogs. The black hounds are interwoven with Wiltshire legend. Susceptible imaginations accounted for many more sightings than in the days of Arthur Shuttlewood's UFOs. Dogs seemed to materialise and vanish as county dwellers from these earlier generations became obsessed with the ghostly barks.

The dogs were said to belong to highwaymen and to witches. Some were said to drag chains as they panted mysteriously along the

Black dogs haunt the county.

21

country lanes. One popular tale, emanating from the Bishops Cannings area, was of a headless canine. A cyclist near Lyneham also fell from his machine and said: 'It was a black dog that threw me off.' There was no evidence that he'd been on the cider. The size of these ghostly dogs varied in the re-telling. Most of the village people frightened by them appeared unanimous about one thing – the dogs were 'big and evil'.

There was not anything evil about the White Birds of Salisbury Plain. Popular legend implied that they looked rather like albatrosses. Not that too many actually saw the birds, which was rather a pity. Our modern Natural History departments would have been grateful for a little more evidence and documentation. The White Birds were said to drift through the air. They supposedly had wings but didn't use them. And they clearly had a sense of respectful timing: they were more inclined to make an appearance when one of the Bishops of Salisbury was dying.

We can discount a great deal. No-one, for instance, really believes the passed-down accounts of personalised aeronautics by Elmer the Monk, who had such faith in the Almighty that he leapt from the top of the tower of the Abbey at Malmesbury and lived to tell the tale. The guide books inform us, tongue-in-cheek, we hope, that the resourceful Elmer floated for a furlong and had no more damage to the human fuselage than a couple of broken limbs.

Malmesbury has a long and envied history. It was a British settlement long before Saxon times. The historic town has every right to parade its legends. If the daring Monk of Malmesbury predated the invention of the aeroplane, so be it . . .'

We are apt, when we think of Wiltshire, to visualise mentally all those rolling downs and the vast, chalky acres without even the sign of a farmhouse, and forget the woodlands. The once royal Savernake Forest, now leased to the Forestry Commission, is renowned for its oaks and beeches. The Grand Avenue of beeches is four miles long and attracts countless admiring visitors. They scuffle contentedly through the fallen leaves, enraptured by the silence of this sylvan sanctuary. Former generations who lived close to Savernake were at

Malmesbury Abbey where Elmer the monk leapt from the top of the tower and lived to tell the tale.

times less enamoured by the tranquility. They would talk of eerie noises – of barks (those black dogs again?) and covens and other unexplained signs of life. There was nothing like the blackness of a forest, criss-crossed by indeterminable tracks, to stir the restive imaginations.

Wiltshire is in a way a victim of its own rich tapestry of history. The wondrous stone monuments act as the starting point for the absorbing business of probing the imponderable. For century after century, lonely shepherds were left only with their sheep, their tormented thoughts and their apparitions.

The guide books will tell you of the second Lord Weymouth of Longleat who, according to rumour, killed his wife's lover and buried the body. Many years later there was indeed a largely decomposed body discovered in the cellar. The ghost of his beautiful wife is said to continue to haunt part of the great house. No public relations officer could ask for more.

Longleat thrives on mystery. We don't even know the name of the architect. Its rooms have since then been occupied by the famous and the bizarre. No-one ever satisfactorily worked out the unconventional lifestyle of the second Lord Weymouth, who spent as little time as he could at Longleat. We must wonder why.

This, in the mischievous tradition of Michael Williams, is another of his evocative books which makes all of us keep wondering why. His miscellany of chapters, all specially commissioned, are full of question marks. We are invited to finish reading – and then to start pondering. There is frankly no reason why we, any more than successive generations of historians and so called experts, should come up with the answers.

In 1984, this Cornish publisher – himself with an insatiable curiosity for the whims and wonders of local history – brought out *Strange Somerset Stories*. The pattern was set. Now he has moved to Wiltshire, where the mysteries multiply by the page. He is an essentially regional publisher. This is the sixth distinct area of the West he has 'explored' and he knows at once that he has unhinged a bulging treasure chest.

The once royal Savernake Forest.

24

About the author
DAVID MUDD

Cornishman David Mudd is Bossiney's most prolific author. He has contributed ten Cornish titles to our list and now writes a chapter on Stonehenge in the first Bossiney title for Wiltshire. Formerly a newspaper journalist, broadcaster and television reporter, he has been Conservative Member of Parliament for Falmouth-Camborne since 1970. His earlier titles 'The Cruel Cornish Sea' and 'Around and About the Roseland' remain in print – and he is currently working on an eleventh Cornish book, 'The River Fal', to be published later in 1989.

David Mudd

Stonehenge
by David Mudd

AS the watery but richly-coloured sun rises on a summer's morn, it lights the mist-shrouded dew-kissed shapes that punctuate the orderliness of earth and seem to sup the first early unfolding land-carpeting rays. On a winter's day, as the wind bites and beats its way from the north, those same shapes take on a new identity, like rugged seafarers impervious to the discomfort of drifting and penetrating rain. And they stand, in the confused kaleidoscope of falling and fallen snow, like proud sentinels unaware of human chill, proud, erect, ageless, vigilant.

It was Rudyard Kipling who kept 'six honest serving men' who taught him all he knew. Their names, although not necessarily in that order, were How? Where? When? Why? What? and Who? Six precise questions designed to add a six-dimensional interrogation to every presumed fact, and to create as near an absolute awareness as possible.

In the case of Stonehenge, the Where? the What? and the When? are well-known. Firstly, the geography is known since the large 'congregation' of standing stones surrounded by an earthwork is set some eight miles to the north of Salisbury. The What? is covered by its undisputed use as, among other things, a receptacle for the remains of the dead. As for the When?, its creation, change and development began almost four thousand years ago.

But what of the Who? who built and used it; and How? was it built; and Why?

Therein lie the ingredients of Wiltshire's greatest riddle.

In trying to answer those questions and thus solve the full mystery, we have to encounter an invading tribe with a name more in keeping with kitchenware than construction; a powerful religious

group who were judges and teachers as well as theological leaders; an ancient king; an Elizabethan map-maker; a distinguished antiquary who sometimes invented yarns to give his findings a bit of sparkle; a few corpses trussed up like oven-ready chickens; and the likes and dislikes of Julius Caesar and the attitudes of Roman armies of occupation.

Julius Caesar, from this tangle of witnesses and red-herrings, is a good starting point since he profoundly observed that 'Gaul as a whole is divided into three parts.' For, indeed, Stonehenge as we know it today was also created in three main parts, with the last one being an amalgam of three distinct stages.

The first work on Stonehenge – its name literally means a monument including 'hanging' stones which, because of their balance on uprights, appear to hang in the air when seen from some angles – began about the year 1800 BC and was basically an outer circular ring and bank with an inner ring of 56 holes. These are known as the 'Aubrey holes' after the seventeenth century antiquary who found them and who, incidentally, was possibly responsible for adding colourful myth to genuine mystery some three-and-a-half thousand years after Stonehenge had been completed to the stage that now remains.

The holes and the enclosed area obviously served as some form of sacred area, a kind of temple-circle-cum-graveyard-cum-crematorium where the ashes of the cremated dead were carefully placed in bags, the neck of which was secured by a pin made of bone. In the centre of the original compound stood the Hele (or 'heel') Stone, a 35 ton block of sarsen sandstone standing at the commanding point marking the head of a major avenue leading in from an entrance at the north-eastern edge of the outer earthwork.

For upwards of a century things must have remained very much as they were, with earthwork predominating over stonework and very few permanent structures. Then, however, the Beaker folk arrived.

The Beakers took their name from the distinctive bell-shaped vessels from which they drank and had begun their civilisation in Spain before moving upwards into France and then fanning outwards into Holland, Germany and into southern England. Their main contribution to the development of early Britain was that they had already mastered the retrieval and use of copper for tools and weapons and were to lead the way into the Bronze Age.

Prehistoric man's engineering skills have stood the test of time at Stonehenge.

Having reached England, they proceeded to occupy much of Wessex. By the standards of the day, they had a positive culture and were religious. They were vigorous, strong and imaginative and were natural farmers. Unlike the other tribes, they did not favour multiple burials. Getting away from the mass graves of others, they gave each corpse an individual resting place – each equipped for the hereafter with a selection of goods, tools and weapons, and laid in a single pit under a single small mound.

Perhaps the farming tradition led to the way the corpses were prepared for burial, with knees drawn upwards and into the chest and arms locking the finished cadaver into something looking like a human version of a trussed chicken on its way to the oven.

The Beaker folk 'inherited' the first phase of Stonehenge and decided to modify their acquisition as well as to add to it. Although they are described as 'short, powerful, ugly and with round heads and prominent foreheads', the Beakers obviously had a natural eye for architectural composition and accuracy as well as having a basic capacity for civil engineering works and techniques. They were able to lift massive blocks of stone to a height of seven metres or more before setting them squarely on pre-erected uprights, relying on the fusion of weight with support to provide a disaster-free arch able to withstand slippage of altered alignment due to settlement.

Their architectural and geometrical qualities can be seen because Stonehenge appears to be based on a series of complex but identifiable triangles and circles, thus suggesting that at least one of the intentions of the builders was that the finished structure could be used for the observation of astronomical phenomena.

The second stage of development started with the task of finding the type and location of suitable materials. Searching throughout the vast areas they occupied, the Beakers came across the ruins of an earlier sacred circle in the Prescelly Mountains of Pembrokeshire. These offered limitless quantities of bluestone merely waiting to be trundled some 330 kilometres or so to the new project. These would be erected in a double circle. To facilitate the final movement of stone to site, the Heel Stone ditch was dug and then filled in again as an access route to the central area. Significantly, in the light of later controversy in the legends of Stonehenge, the lay-out was designed in such a way that, at dawn on Midsummer's Day, the rising sun would send its rays directly into the central circle.

Sadly, the Beakers may have bitten-off more than they could chew either in time, in skill or in materials, for after almost a century of work, they had still not completed their task and, indeed, some of what they had achieved was carefully reversed by later developers when the third phase began.

Around 1500 BC, a refurbishment, redesign and remodelling took place. This time the materials chosen were very much more to hand, lying in the sarsen stone deposits of – comparatively - nearby Marlborough. A total of 80 blocks were each hauled some 50 kilometres across country from the Marlborough Downs to be set up in a ring of 30 uprights capped by an unbroken circle of stone lintels to create a resulting structure unique among contemporary British and western European monuments. The stones were some ten metres long and weighed, on average, 30 tons apiece.

Each block was worked upon by teams of craftsmen until its surfaces were as smooth as the skill of the dressers and their primitive tools could make them. Each of the lintels appears to have been

32

Perhaps Wiltshire's greatest mystery – Stonehenge.

individually shaped and cut for its exact place in the upper capping.

For some reason that has never been fully explained, the underlying thrust of design and construction seems to have been influenced by styles of roughly the same era in Greece and Crete, with some of the more detailed carvings having a close similarity. Inside the 'enclosed' circle of capped uprights, the builders set a horseshoe-shaped formation of five larger arches with an altar stone at the centre.

The second stage of the third phase was one of the first recorded examples of the successful recycling of strategic materials!

Using the Pembrokeshire bluestone brought by the Beaker folk but dismantled by fellow Wessex workers a century earlier, a new team (1500-1400 BC) dressed and reshaped the dismantled bluestones and re-set them, in a different form, in yet another concentric circle. They dug – but abandoned – two other series of holes as if the original intention was that the central altar stone should eventually be guarded by at least four sets of outer standing circles of one sort or another. Perhaps, as in schemes some 3,000 years later, either ingenuity, resources or resolve petered out.

Undaunted by whatever had been the reason, 1400 BC saw the completion of the final works on Stonehenge. The much-travelled and redeployed bluestones were given, after some 400 years, a permanent resting place. Having been disturbed yet again, they were re-set to form the bluestone circle and horseshoe that remain today and have miraculously withstood the combined and individual assaults of time, weather and vandals for over 3,000 changeless years of unflinching immobility.

But history, myth, magic and mystery did not end with the completion of Britain's most famous, dramatic and unique primitive stone monument.

It is suggested that the most monumental myth-maker of them all was the antiquary, John Aubrey, who lived from 1626-1697 and who may have put forward the Druid-associated theme by way of a joke.

Certainly there is a popular belief that the Druids attached great importance to Stonehenge before and during Roman times. This line of argument has a reasoned and reasonable basis in that the Druids would have been the natural successors to the original creators of what had obviously been built as a centre for religious rites. The belief also prayed-in-aid that the Druids were sun-worshippers and that their catching the first rays of the sun on Midsummer's Day was of deep importance.

Traditionally the Druids taught philosophy and astronomy; they cremated their dead; they made human sacrifice; they used hill-tops, springs, open groves and open spaces.

Since Stonehenge has a reputed 'slaughter stone'; has revealed cremated remains; indicates the practises associated with culture, religion, astronomy and astrology; and fits the landscape requirements, then it would seem to fit and answer the circumstantial demands of Druidic presence.

However, the greatest authority on the Druids was Julius Caesar himself. And to put it bluntly, he could do without them. Their culture, their leadership, their influence and their gods ran contrary to the interests of Rome. He repressed them throughout Gaul and England and had their monuments destroyed.

The fact that there is no trace of any Roman attempt to destroy or obliterate Stonehenge would seem to suggest that the Romans had regarded it as Druid-free in their eyes and era.

An old picture postcard of Stonehenge. Clearly there was a more casual approach to its preservation in those days by the flimsy little ring of wire around it.

But, perhaps more tellingly, no real mention of the Druid connection seems to exist prior to John Aubrey. It was he who, in 1685, completed 'an unpublished discourse on Stonehenge' in which he floated the Druid theory. While he was undoubtedly a scholar of distinction, he admits that his work on researching the monument was 'tumultuarily stitched-up' suggesting some haste and a lack of proof that, perhaps, led to the book not finding a patron or a publisher.

'My head', he wrote, 'was always working, never idle, and even travelling did glean some observations some whereof are to be valued.'

The only book he ever published himself was a highly entertaining collection of tales of the supernatural and ghost stories. It was said that he was 'a good retailer of anecdotes and his head teams with particulars ... half the charm is in his simple credulity.'

Sadly, then, the Druids might have been a colourful creation of

35

that credulity; the subject of a good anecdote; or merely an unresearched utterance leading to fantasy regarded as fact.

Certainly more recent authorities do not follow John Aubrey and tend to distance themselves from the Druids. Warning that Druidic rituals and worship *could* have taken place, they advise that such associations should be treated with caution. Perhaps the most open attitude of all comes from the expert who suggests that 'while it is not impossible that some of the ceremonies performed there were solar or astronomical, its connection with the Druids is a popular misconception.'

But the greatest challenge to the Aubrey claim lies in the writings of another researcher who was undoubtedly diligent rather than dilletante in his preparation – John Speed.

John Speed compiled a map and history of Wiltshire some 70 years ahead of John Aubrey. His maps are artistic as well as authoritative, visual as well as geographical, educational as well as academic. Traditionally he decorated the map of each county he surveyed with the coats-of-arms of the major families plus the one small self-indulgence of illustrating and highlighting a local feature that caught his attention.

In the case of his map of Wiltshire, John Speed allocated the greatest space and detail to Stonehenge than to any other noted feature of any other English county.

What he wrote of Stonehenge is so captivating but so detailed that it is always worthy of recollection:

'Aurelius Ambrosus buryed at Stonheng Anno 500.

'This ancient monument was erected by Aurelius surnamed Ambrosus King of ye Brittaines, whose nobility in the raigne of Vortiger (his countrye's scourge) about ye yere of Christ 457 by treachery of ye Saxons, on a daye of parley were there slaughtered and their Bodyes there interred. In memory of whereof this King Aurel: caused this Trophy to be set up. Admirable to posterityes Both in forme and quantyte. The matter thereof are stones of great bigness conteyning twenty eighte foot and more in length and tenn in breadth these are set in ye ground by tower 2, and a third laide gatewise over thwart fastned with tenons and mortaises wrought in the same, very dangerous to all that pass thereunder. The forme is round, and as it seemeth, has been circulated with three ranks of these stones, many of which are now fallen down, and the uttermost standing contayneth in compass three hundred feet by measure.

36

The great stone circle of Stonehenge rising on the skyline.

'They are roughe and of a graye colour standing within a trench that hath bene much deeper. In this place the foresayd King Aurelius with 2 more of ye British kings, his successors, have been buryed with many more of their nobilitye and in this place, under little banks to this date, are found by digging ye bones of mighty men and Armour of large and ancient fashion.'

John Speed was, like most visitors to Stonehenge, immensely moved by its atmosphere, its history, its image. His research would have involved using many of the sources available to John Aubrey yet he did not mention the Druids.

Surely, then, despite the modern Midsummer rite when, as the

sun rises and shines towards Stonehenge and a Druidic priest intones: 'We seek and find Thee in the glory of the dawn. We seek and find Thee when the darkness of the night has fled. The sleep of faith has ever led through night to dawn', the celebration must be that of a ritualistic tradition far removed from the foundations of fact.

And so Stonehenge remains a mystery. The When? the Where? the What? the How? may be known, but the Why? and the real Who? are hidden by time, camouflaged in myth, enshrined in folklore.

But, as Sir Arthur Conan Doyle once wrote: 'When you have eliminated the impossible, whatever remains, however improbable, must be nearer the truth.'

And at that prehistoric and awesome place with its sixteen standing and various scattered stones, a great truth *does* exist. But it is a full truth that can only become a mystery solved when the impossible is finally eliminated by a depth of knowledge that is still denied us.

Despite the modern midsummer rite Stonehenge remains a mystery.

39

About the author
POLLY LLOYD

Polly Lloyd is a well-known voice on Westcountry radio. She lives in Bristol with her husband, two children, two cats and two goldfish. A Scorpio subject, she was born in Liverpool and came to Bristol at the age of fourteen, when her family moved to the city. Polly Lloyd joined BBC Radio Bristol in 1981. She is currently presenting the Teatime Show, each weekday afternoon. Her interests include the theatre, dance and opera, and history in any shape or form. In 1987 she visited Egypt and produced and presented a BBC Radio Bristol cassette on Ancient Egypt and Egypt today. In 1988 Polly Lloyd made her debut for Bossiney with 'Legends of Dorset'. She is currently working on 'Strange Stories', also to be published by Bossiney.

Polly Lloyd

Wiltshire Folklore
by Polly Lloyd

ONE of the best descriptions of legend I have ever read came from fellow Bossiney author Sally Jones who saw legend as 'gossip grown old'. How right she is, for legend is really the stories that men have told to each other, to their children and their grandchildren. Stories that explained the ways of the world, that told of the people who lived and loved and worked roundabout, stories of gods and ghosts. Gossip, of course, is notorious for embellishing the facts and critics dismiss it because of this, but it is well worth searching for the grain of truth, for often legend carries an ancient wisdom.

In Wiltshire, past and present, fact and folklore all combine to paint a richer picture for those willing to linger and look deeper.

The landscape itself is a perfect setting for legend – the chalk uplands, Salisbury Plain to the south, Marlborough Downs to the north, magnificent prehistoric treasures like Stonehenge and Avebury. History relates the facts, pencilling in the outline, as it were. But legend and folklore add colour and texture to an otherwise stark canvas. Listen to the legend and the folklore, and you will learn about the personality of the place.

For many people it is the ancient legend of Wiltshire that is the most fascinating. The country is rich in evidence of earlier civilisations – primitive in comparison to ours in so many ways and yet capable of achievements we are still unable to explain. Stonehenge and Avebury are of course the most spectacular examples of those strange and awesome times, and you can read about them elsewhere in this book. But there are other places too well worth visiting.

Just south of Avebury, for example, not far from the River Kennet, is Silbury Hill, generally acknowledged to be the largest man-made

Silbury Hill, generally acknowledged to be the largest man-made hill in Europe.

hill in Europe. It is remarkably large, covering about five acres and rising 130 feet into the air. It is made from chalk rubble but how and why is a matter of some speculation. Scientific research is fairly inconclusive, able only to suggest that Silbury Hill was not built as a burial mound because as yet no hard evidence of burials has been discovered, despite numerous investigations.

Folklore, happily, is much more forthcoming. According to legend, Silbury is the final resting place of King Sil, or Zel as his name is pronounced in local dialect. Some say he was buried in a golden coffin, others that he was buried upright in the saddle of his horse, a king in golden armour riding his faithful steed into the afterlife. Since 1776, people have periodically carried out excavations in search of Sil and his treasure but no-one has ever found it, although the king sometimes rides around the hill at night, his golden armour glinting in the moonlight.

Incidentally, Wiltshire folklore tells of more buried treasure – a golden coffin at Winkelbury Hill, Berwick St John, a golden chair at the round barrow at Enford, and a golden wheelbarrow – what a wonderful image that conjures up – at Barrow Lane, Littleton Drew. Searching for the treasure however can be a perilous business. A contemporary account of an excavation at Silbury Hill led by Dean Mereweather of Hereford in 1849 tells of a 'dramatic high Gothick thunderstorm'. The Dean himself described it as the most spectacular storm he had ever witnessed, making the 'hills re-echo in the crashing peals, and Silbury itself . . . tremble to its base.' The locals apparently were not in the least bit surprised, but as the author of the account somewhat dismissively relates, they were 'not divested of superstitious dread.'

There are other explanations about the origins of Silbury Hill, and these involve that indefatigable landscaper, the Devil. The stories differ on points of detail but they are the same in essence: the Devil, filled with vengeance, set off to bury some Wiltshire town under a layer of earth but was thwarted and flung away the earth in a fit of pique, thereby creating Silbury.

One version tells of great rivalry between the people of Marlborough and the people of Devizes which culminated in a bitter row. The Devil sided with the Marlborough lot and set off to Devizes, determined to obliterate it with a load of earth. Luckily for Devizes, the people there heard that he was coming and turned for help to St John who by chance was in the neighbourhood. His advice was unusual but effective. The townspeople gathered up all their worn-out boots, put them in a sack and gave them to an old man who set off to meet the Devil. The Devil meanwhile was growing weary and ill-tempered because he was carrying a huge mound of earth in his apron. When he saw the old man he asked him how far it was to Devizes. 'Well,' said the old man, 'I left there three years ago, and look, these are all the boots I've worn out along the way.' The Devil's loyalty to Marlborough vanished on hearing this, and with a mighty roar he flung down the earth, creating Silbury Hill.

A variation on this theme claims that the Devil's target was Avebury. Legend has it that he tolerated Avebury as a centre of worship, but his patience snapped when Stonehenge was built. All

44

Horses figure largely in Wiltshire's history. It is racehorse country now but even in folklore those noble beasts thundered across the Downs. King Sil, whose final resting place is Silbury Hill, is said by some to have been buried upright in the saddle of his horse, a king in golden armour riding his faithful steed into the afterlife.

this religion was too much for him so he took his spade and dug a great slice out of Salisbury Plain, intending to smother Avebury with it. Once again his plans were foiled, this time by the priests who used their prayers and spells to stop him. Thoroughly frustrated, he threw down the spadeful of earth, and Silbury Hill was the result.

However Silbury came to be, it is a place that has drawn people to it down the years. In the eighteenth and early nineteenth centuries, villagers from Avesbury celebrated Palm Sunday by walking in procession to the top of Silbury to eat fig cakes and drink sugared water. The hill would be crowded with people. Similarly right up until the early days of this century, villagers used to climb Cley Hill near Warminster, also on Palm Sunday, and there within the walls of the prehistoric earthworks they joined in a game played with sticks and balls. Martinsell Hill near Pewsey was also the scene of a procession of villagers, from Wootton Rivers and other nearby places.

Wiltshire people have long enjoyed festivals, Christian or pagan or a happy blend of both. May Queens abounded throughout the county, and the custom of young girls carrying garlands of flowers from house to house existed in varying forms in many places. The young ladies would cajole pennies from people, usually to be spent at nearby fairs. Singing, dancing and generally enjoying oneself were common factors. Maypoles, of course, were very much a part of the tradition, until the days of Cromwell, when they were viewed with great distaste as pagan symbols by the Puritans. Sadly, many villages failed to resurrect their maypoles after the Restoration in 1660.

The hobby horse was also part of the mayday celebrations and in Salisbury Museum you can still see the famous Salisbury Hob-nob. You will also find there the Salisbury Giant, a marvellous creation some twelve feet high, dark and swarthy with a beard. He was carried through the streets by a man hidden underneath his flowing robes. The Giant dates back many years; records show that Henry VII and his Queen saw him in 1496. He played a part in all the major celebrations – St John's Night – Midsummer Night – St Osmund's Night and St Peter's Night, and he was sometimes referred to as St Christopher.

Folklore tells of buried treasure – a golden wheelbarrow at Littleton Drew.

46

During the nineteenth century the Giant and Hob-nob were often seen in processions in Salisbury, processions that by all accounts were fairly rowdy, involving frequent stops for liquid refreshment.

In Victorian times, most Wiltshire villages had a village club. These clubs were a simple form of friendly society, a sort of insurance scheme, dues being paid weekly and members getting sick pay when they fell ill and could not work. They were also known as slate clubs, the accounts being kept on a slate at the village inn. At the end of the year, the slate was wiped clean and any surplus used to pay for a treat for all, which as you can imagine invariably ended up with the majority of members pretty drunk.

More often than not, the club year ended at Whitsuntide, a convenient time to choose because it was already a day for celebration. In this way the tradition of festivals, feasts and revels was adopted and adapted. The ancient pagan festivals, dating from the days when the old gods were worshipped, were taken over by the new believers to mark the high points of the Christian year. The church holy-days in turn took on a more secular significance, or were simply used as an excuse for a good old-fashioned knees-up. When the temperance movement saw what a large part drink played in these holidays, it determined to win people away from the evils of alcohol by organising the Sunday School anniversaries on Whit Monday.

One of Wiltshire's best known traditions takes place each year at Wishford on Oak Apple Day – May 29th. The celebrations begin before dawn when a tin-pan band armed with bin-lids, shovels, drums, recorders, anything, indeed, guaranteed to make a noise, work their way through the village waking everyone up. Then it's off to Grovely Forest, high on the ridge between the Wylye and Nader valleys. The purpose is to cut fresh young green boughs from the oak trees with which to decorate one's home. A prize is given to the best-decorated house, and another to the bearer of the branch with the most oak-apples. Then everyone goes home for breakfast.

Shortly after ten a group of villagers set off for Salisbury Cathedral, where they offer their boughs and branches to the Dean and give the traditional cry 'Grovely! Grovely! Grovely! And all Grovely!' Mission accomplished, they return to lunch with the mayors of Salisbury and Wilton and various other local dignitaries. The rest of the day is taken up with a typical English fête.

Now clearly all this is great fun – for those who like getting up early – and it is a marvellous tourist attraction but strange customs

48

like this do not simply spring up overnight. So what are the origins of the Wishford Oak Apple Day? A little investigation shows that it is a classic example of the multi-purpose festival.

Some 200 years ago the local landowner, the Earl of Pembroke, tried to prevent the villagers of Wishford from collecting green oak branches in Grovely Forest. There was uproar, and eventually the Earl was forced to give way. Some people believe the Oak Apple Day festivities commemorate that victory. But it would seem that the villagers fought so hard to retain their rights to the forest because collecting the green boughs was already a custom. And indeed a document written at the time of the Dissolution of the monasteries during the reign of Henry VIII declares that the villagers had the right to gather wood in the forest, to graze cattle and pigs there and to kill one fat buck every Whitsuntide. It also mentions that the villagers would visit the cathedral at 'New Sarum' each Whit Tuesday and lay claim to their rights to the forest by shouting 'Grovely! Grovely! Grovely! And all Grovelly!' And so we learn that a custom still continued in the twentieth century, shown on television, recorded on film and video, captured in countless snapshots, was already a part of Wiltshire life 400 years ago in the sixteenth century.

Naturally, the county of Wiltshire can boast its fair share of intriguing characters. As well as King Sil, some people believe that King Lud, the reputed founder of London, once lived in a castle at Ludgershall, although others dispute this. King Ina, king of Wessex from 688 – 726, is said to have fought the Mercians at Adam's Grave near Sidbury in 715. And King Alfred the Great is supposed to have had his legendary mishap with the cakes at Brixton Deverill.

In Sherston the local inn is named after a hero of bygone days called John Rattlebone; some say a small carved figure in the church is an image of him. Rattlebone evidently fought valiantly in a great battle between the Saxons and the Danes in the early part of the eleventh century. He was badly wounded in the stomach but fought on, pausing only to snatch up a tile which luckily was to hand, pressing it firmly against the gash to staunch the blood. In recognition of his bravery he was given the manor of Sherston:

> *Fight well, Rattlebone,*
> *Thou shalt have Sherston.*

Tradition claims that a medieval wooden chest, carved with the initials R.B. and found in the parish church once held John Rattlebone's armour.

49

During the nineteenth century there were some rowdy traditional processions around Salisbury's gracious streets.

In the southern part of Wiltshire, at Wishford – of Oak Apple Day fame – a fifteenth century knight called Sir Thomas Bonham is commemorated in the church. Sir Thomas was not a wealthy knight and as his family grew and his responsibilities increased, he began to despair of his financial situation. When his wife gave birth to twins it was the last straw and he set off to do what all good knights should do – fight for glory on a foreign battle field.

Seven years later he returned to Wishford. Nobody recognised him at first because he was dressed as a pilgrim and furthermore, legend has it, he had let his beard grow ever since leaving Wiltshire. Fortunately, he was wearing a special ring which proved to his wife that her husband had indeed come home and she welcomed him with great delight. So delighted was she, in fact, that in the fullness of time, she gave birth to seven babies all at once. The gallant and pious Sir Thomas' efforts to limit the size of his family were a miserable failure. The babies were carried to Wishford church in a sieve to be christened, and this used to be commemorated in the annual Oak Apple Day procession when seven dolls were carried.

In 1413 the young lord of the manor of Langley Burrell died for his beliefs. He was Reginald de Cobham, a follower of the antipapist John Wycliffe. It was a time of religious fervour and Wycliffe's teachings were regarded as heretical. Poor Reginald was taken to the top of Steinbrook Hill, stripped naked and burnt at the stake. His ghost is said to haunt the hill on moonlit nights, still naked and curiously, carrying his head under his arm.

Lacock Abbey, now owned by the National Trust and one of Wiltshire's most delightful tourist attractions has many stories to tell. In the late sixteenth century the daughter of the house, Olive Sharrington, fell in love with a Worcestershire fellow called John Talbot. Her parents were against the match and poor Olive gave up all hope of ever being allowed to marry him. Heartbroken, she threw herself off the abbey battlements, preferring death to an unhappy life. Two things saved her. Firstly, her petticoats billowed out so that she floated rather than fell to earth, and secondly, she landed on top of her true love, almost killing him in fact. Luckily they both survived. Her father, conceding defeat, is reputed to have said 'Since she made such leaps she should e'en marry him' and the young lovers lived happily ever after.

The young woman who gave birth to a baby boy one wild and stormy night in 1575 was less fortunate. The local midwife Mother

Barnes was woken in the night by a masked man who wanted her to attend a confinement. He paid her well, but insisted that she should travel blindfold. He took her to a large house some seven or eight miles away where she delivered the child. As soon as the baby was born, far from rejoicing at its safe arrival, the mysterious stranger snatched the child from its mother and threw it into the blazing fire. Ignoring the distraught mother's screams, he blindfolded the protesting midwife once more and she was taken home.

The cruel masked man might have got away with this appalling act had it not been for the quick wit of Mother Barnes. She managed to cut off a small piece of material from the bed hangings in the fateful room, and she also counted the number of stairs. The next day she went straight to the magistrates and before long they had tracked down the culprit – 'Wild' William Darrell of Littlecote House near Chilton Foliat. But Darrell was not without influence and, despite Mother Barnes' evidence against him, he was acquitted.

However, the brutal death of the innocent baby did not go unavenged. Some time later, Darrell was out hunting when his horse suddenly reared up and threw him. He was killed instantly. According to legend, the horse had been frightened by an apparition of a burning child. The spot is still called 'Darrell's Stile' and Darrell's ghost is said to haunt it. The baby's wretched mother, said by some to be Darrell's own sister, haunts the house.

Wiltshire has its ghosts – it also has its witches. As David Foot suggests in his opening chapter of this book, the distinction between wicked witch and eccentric old lady is hard to define and the blame for many an unexplained happening in many a village was laid at the door of many a harmless, if unpopular, spinster. Tales of these women are full of mystery and magic.

Stories of Lydia Shears, whom David mentions, tells of how the village poachers would bribe her with tobacco and snuff to attract hares for them to catch. She teased one farmer to distraction by turning herself into a hare which he would chase with his dogs only to have the hare disappear into thin air in Lydia Shears' garden. The farmer grew so frustrated by this that he turned to the local vicar for advice. This good man of the cloth suggested shooting the hare with a bullet fashioned from a silver sixpence. The next time the mischievous animal taunted him, the farmer did exactly that – soon after Lydia Shears was found dead in her cottage with a silver bullet in her heart.

Animals, magical hares included, feature a great deal in Wiltshire folklore; appropriately in a county that boasts so many white horses cut into the chalk hillsides. Dogs that howled, owls that hooted and cats that upped and left the house were all said to foretell death. Similarly, rats and mice and even that otherwise friendly little bird the robin were all considered to be bad omens if they entered a home. Ghostly animals have been seen haunting the countryside – black dogs, donkeys, horses and pigs. The cockerel, significant in folklore in many places, plays its part in Wiltshire too; in Hill Deverell in the late 1800s the cocks crowed through the night, crowing the number of the hour, which must have meant sleepless nights for the locals. Shrews were believed to be capable of bewitching cattle, and hedgehogs of sucking milk from cows as they lay in the fields.

And so you will see that the county of Wiltshire, whose history unfolds layer by layer way back to ancient times, is rich in folklore, rich and enriching. Any traveller willing to leave the busy highways and take instead the quiet country roads, to pause beside the great houses and wander through the villages, to linger and to listen will find the time and effort amply rewarded. So many wonders to marvel at, so many mysteries to ponder over and so many tales to hear. Tales that Wiltshire folk have talked about for years, for remember, legend is only 'gossip grown old'.

What a wonderful tapestry it weaves.

About the author
NOEL WELCH

Noel Welch was born in London and educated at Parsons Mead, Ashtead and St Hilda's College, Oxford. She has travelled in Africa, France and Spain and had a studio for two years in St Ives. She lives at Manaton on Dartmoor. Her poems have appeared in the P.E.N. Anthology 'New Poems 1961', 'Best Poems of 1957' and poetry magazines such as 'Outposts'. She has published two books of verse, 'Ten Poems' and 'Witness'. In Cornwall she is well remembered for her brilliant features in 'The Cornish Review' on such creative characters as the du Maurier sisters, potter Bernard Leach and sculptor Dame Barbara Hepworth. This is Noel Welch's first contribution to the Bossiney list.

Noel Welch

Avebury

by Noel Welch

THE first time I saw Avebury was at 8.00 am one foggy January morning. I had missed the road to Calne and did not know where I was when a presence more than an object loomed ahead. The road gently curved away from it but not before I had sensed further on another mysterious shape. As I neared the fog thinned enough for me to see they were both huge rocks. With only the dimmest knowledge of Avebury and its stone circle I stopped and reached for my map.

I had left Devon at 5.00 am without so much as a cup of coffee and for the past hour had been driving in ever worsening conditions. I was slightly light-headed and completely disorientated. In short in a mood to imagine things. Having lived for 30 years on Dartmoor I am used to odd shaped rocks but these stones had a completely different feel. As I sat snug in my Landrover the fog rolled back leaving the nearest stone clearly visible. I had plenty of time to absorb every detail of its contour before the stone behind it was similarly unwrapped.

I got out and walked from one to the other touching them, leaning against them and recalling how the sculptor Barbara Hepworth once told me she liked people to touch her work, to experience it physically. These stones were not carved or worked, they were natural shapes but they felt handled. There was no other living thing in sight, no bird, no cow, no rabbit, just blurred sky, grass and stone. I had never felt more ephemeral; the stones the only permanence – past, present, future.

Suddenly an impatient snort from my trailer, announcing the

'These stones were not carved or worked, they were natural shapes but they felt handled.'

mare I was taking to stud wanted her breakfast, recalled me to the business I was about. After several wrong turnings I eventually found the road but instead of visualising the progeny of this carefully planned union, thoughts that would normally occupy me at the end of such a journey, I experienced what I can only describe as a long haunting. I opened the window and was driving as fast as I could along the narrow lane leading me to my destination when a man on a tractor cutting a hedge in the brutal way practised nowadays brought me to a halt. One of us had got to back. Thanking him when finally he reversed into a gateway close behind him I heard myself saying: 'I have just come from Avebury', and found he had strong opinions as to what should be done 'with them there stones'.

Back home, and deep in all the relevant literature I could lay my hands on, I discovered that my hedge-cutter could have been a reincarnation of one of those eighteenth century labourers who so infuriated Dr Stukeley – the first scholar to properly document Avebury – because, whenever they needed a stone to make a bridge or reinforce a barn they simply helped themselves to one of Avebury's or, worse still, when they wanted more land to plough, overturned and smashed them. I also discovered that the stones I had seen were part of the largest stone circle in England. Stonehenge is more dramatic. Avebury, in spite of, perhaps because of, the village that has grown up 'around and within it', is more mysterious.

Stone circles called Dom Rings or Thing Steads in Scandinavia and Cromlechs in France are made up of 'unhewn stone set up in a roughly circular shape usually on level ground'. And like the small circles found on Dartmoor, they are nearly always old burial grounds – the chambered cairns of the Stone Age. Bronze Age circles are usually smaller because then it was only the burnt bones or ashes that were buried, sometimes in an upright pot, sometimes covered by an inverted one. There is no conclusive proof, and one must remember this, that the Great Circles like Avebury and Stonehenge or Stennis in Orkney had a different origin but many people feel they did, feelings should never be wholly ignored.

Avebury is alluded to in a charter of King Athelstan dated 939 AD. William Aubrey wrote an account of it in 1663 for Charles II and Inigo Jones depored the removal of rocks both from Stonehenge and Avebury before Dr Stukeley condemned its plundering in 1740. In 1820 Sir Richard Hoare examined it for his Ancient Wiltshire.

There is more though to Avebury, or Abury as it was once called, than its circle which is its main feature. There is also a rampart, a ditch and two mysterious avenues. The rampart or bank is on the outside, then comes the ditch. Both of them have four entrances and enclose some 28 acres. The ditch, now silted up and eroded, was once wide and deep with steep sides and a flat bottom. One butt end, noted for being so neatly squared off, must surely be among the earliest examples of tidying up on record. The earth dug out of the ditch with picks made from the antlers of red deer was hauled to the surface in wicker baskets and piled on the outside to make the rampart. Inside rampart and ditch, and following more or less the same line – none of the circumferences are perfect – is the stone circle itself which once consisted of one hundred unquarried stones or sarsens. Inside this, there were originally two smaller circles. Only four stones of one survive – two upright, two fallen – though their positioning suggests there were once 27, with three stones called The Cove in the centre. None of the other's probable 29 stones, with a central very tall one called The Obelisk, are now standing.

It is the standing stones that obsess me. Photographs of them cover all the walls of my usually rather bare study and look at me from open books – carried back from libraries or given me by friends – which lie on every available table and chair.

It was the absolute 'thereness' of the standing stones that made my second visit. And, looking at them in the flat light of that mid-summer day, how they got there seemed almost as remarkable as their survival.

They came from the chalk downs to the east where lots of stones still lie on the surface as they do on Dartmoor – a constant hazard hunting, but on the downs near Marlborough, instead of granite rocks, they are remnants of a thin layer of sandstone laid down over the chalk.

How were they transported? On sledges? On rollers? How many were crippled moving them? How many killed? What herbs were applied to crushed hands, legs, feet? What potions given to dull the pain? How many widows silently cursed these rocks? Were the dead given decent burial or, regarded as so much natural waste, disposed of as quickly as possible so as not to discourage co-workers? What motives, what dreams inspired their overseers? We shall never know. All is conjecture, surmise.

I keep using the words probably, possibly, could, if, perhaps – they are unavoidable. We know only what we have and see – the stones themselves and the dug up evidence preserved in the local museum – pots, shards, arrowheads, pieces of wicker and horn and, inevitably, bones. The stones vary in shape and size and no attempt seems to have been made at a uniform height but long narrow stones often alternate with short wedge-shaped ones and could represent male and female forms. Extra large stones, too, mark the entrances to the avenues, some weighing 40 tons or more. One understands why none of them were carved, just getting them here was achievement enough. They are left to tell, or not to tell, their own story.

Who dared move these monuments! The Church dared. Until the Norman Conquest, except for those stones the Church removed for building its own place of worship, most of them seem to have remained intact but long before Dr Stukeley's bitter condemnation of local labourers, and bitter it was – 'This stupendous fabric ... which left to itself would have lasted as long as the globe itself has fallen a sacrifice to the wretched ignorance and avarice of a little village unluckily placed within it' – the Church had begun demolishing what it regarded as an unchristian place. The Church has given us more than it removed but it removed a lot. Its buildings were often erected on pagan sites but when it grew more powerful what it could not take over or adapt it destroyed.

Avebury's stones were regularly overturned, probably, we are told, with some pomp, as a warning to successive generations not to hanker after strange gods whose cults often persisted here as they did in France. The Inquisition found that as a child Joan of Arc had with other children danced round a magic tree – one more black mark against a girl who in whatever age she had lived would, I think, have been open to influences other than those of the there and then, providing she believed they were good. When a stone was to be felled a pit was dug beside it in which a fire was lighted then quickly extinguished, to set up stresses within the stone which made it easier to smash. At one of these 'ceremonial overturnings' an itinerant surgeon was fatally injured. In his grave together with the tools of his trade were found coins dated AD 1300. Long before these destructive burnings Avebury's stones must have witnessed fire though this was probably the first time flames had been aimed against them.

We have proof of when the surgeon lived but in spite of carbon dating there is no certainty about the date of Avebury. It was probably built between 2,500 and 2,000 BC in late Neolithic times when the Beaker people, named after their pottery, were coming over from the

Sculptor, the late Barbara Hepworth, who said she liked people to touch her work, to experience it physically.

Low Countries. We know the man was a surgeon because of the probe and scissors found in his pocket. Nothing has been found to prove Avebury was once a temple though clearly the Church, or anyway its parishoners, believed it had been.

If it was more than simply a burial place and was not a temple, what was it? A meeting place for barter and exchange of news; a huge market place? It is too vast, too grand for a market. One cannot dismiss the possibility that it was a complex and important graveyard – a certain Mr Ferguson believed that those who fell in the last Arthurian battle at Badon Hill were buried here but I, like many others, believe it was an open temple though to Whom or to What and how that Who or What was worshipped will, I imagine, always

Avebury's puzzling stone-strewn landscape.

remain a mystery. At that time, the sun was manifestly the most obvious thing to worship and is often connected with fertility rites – presumably because of its ripening qualities – which fits in with the alternating male and female shapes of some of the stones. Another reason for believing it was a temple is that archaeologists tell us that the ditch was once filled with water, not as a means of defence but to show one was approaching a special place. No market place would merit such a distinction, a graveyard might.

It has even been suggested that this ditch could be the origin of all moats making them, not obstacles to be overcome, but signs that something valued lay ahead. This is a delightful idea but walking around the earthwork, where here and there I found traces of the platform that once separated rampart and ditch, I thought of another explanation. If this circle had once represented the sun its builders might well have thought it advisable to have water at hand in case one day their symbol also caught fire. A more prosaic reason for the presence of water is that any large gathering of people would need water and if, after all, Avebury was simply a huge market so would their animals.

I visited Avebury for the third time when I was staying with friends at Malmesbury and drove over late one amber afternoon. The trees were more in evidence, the shadows long. The shadows of the stones looked even more solid than the stones themselves. It was the long shadows that pointed me to The Avenues where Dr Stukeley was again my guide – I feel I know Dr Stukeley very well. He made a special study of The Avenues and was the first to realise there were two of them, both passing through the great circle and both stone-lined and that huge stones guarded their four entrances. But just as none of the circles are quite true so none of the entrances or exits are perfectly aligned but whether because of construction difficulties, or purposefully, to confuse evil influences, no one knows. The Kennet Avenue – the Kennet is a small tributary of the Thames – runs south-east and ends in a double stone circle known as the Sanctuary or Serpent's Head on a promontory of Overton Hill called Hac Pen – hac is a name for Serpent, pen means head.

Luckily the good doctor made drawings of the Serpent's Head in 1712, it was destroyed the following year. The north part of this avenue was restored by Alexander Keiller, Avebury's last owner before the National Trust, and in it there is the suggestion of a curve that could represent the Solar Serpent. In Egyptian mythology the

Sun and the Serpent were powerful deities – Dr Stukeley was an authority on Egypt – for a long time other scholars thought the second avenue, which he was convinced ran from the west entrance to and beyond Beckhamton and was therefore called the Beckhamton Avenue, was just the doctor allowing himself to be carried away. They were wrong. Cable layers, not archaeologists, found it in 1968 and it is still waiting to be explored.

The Avenues have a mystery of their own – ways in, ways out; comings, goings; people processing. What people? I shut my eyes and try to imagine them. I see nothing. The stones are cabalistic, enigmatic but on that golden autumn evening, with only a few locals around, I felt strange stirrings, movement that was nothing to do with me, but which for a moment swept me along as lightly and firmly as a wind.

The Church that destroyed many pagan sites it could not absorb or reshape met its match at Avebury. These stones still stubbornly defiant speak of the gods behind the God, of man's earliest harkings after some knowledge of from where to where. Before Heaven and Hell were polarized and the Christian Saviour crowned what strange barbaric rites were practised here? The Church has been barbaric enough – to heathens, to heretics, but, whatever took place in this stone ring was, I feel, more elemental – in touch with fire and water, earth and air; with the strength of the lion, the need of the hungry and the hopeless vulnerability of the lamb before the Lamb of God arrived with Its contradictions, complications and Its monstrous claim.

It was dark when I got back to Malmesbury and I was talking about Avebury over a late supper when my patient host suddenly said 'I suppose you know it is on a ley line.' I did not and did not even know whether leys – alignments of ancient sites across – were real or imaginary. As they are mostly invisible I think they are mostly imaginary. Be that as it may, one of Britain's longest leys begins at St Michael's Mount in Cornwall, goes via the Cheesewring on Bodmin Moor to St Michael's Church on Dartmoor then via Glastonbury to Avebury and from there to Bury St Edmunds touching en route hills and churches dedicated to St Michael.

Some people think ley lines are channels for earth energies presumably good ones because St Michael – first in the fight against Satan – seems to have become their Patron Saint. I hope though my study is not about to have maps of ley lines all over its walls as fervently as I hope their influence is strong and good. In the eighteenth century Avebury was partially ruined by 'the ignorant and the avaricious'. It is under similar threat today, but, today, if the many voices now raised in its defence are not heeded, its ruin will be complete.

For a long time Avebury's stones have been comfortably embedded in its village. Now its village must enfold and protect them. Allow vandals on its outskirts, a Goth in one of its ancient houses and the atmosphere surrounding this 'stupendous fabric' will be totally destroyed. Atmosphere is a delicate thing that can often withstand great influxes of people who come to participate in some form of homage, worship, study or celebration. It cannot withstand endless busloads of mindless sightseers. I am not optimistic. Ignorance and greed are always there and, save for a few heroic exceptions, when has any village presented a united front?

For me, the happy owner of a yearling, that will eventually be as white as the white horse carved on a hill in sight of this magic ring, Avebury has opened up another world. Crowd it, commercialise it and it will become just another tourist attraction; one more stop on the list of places to see. Better it means a great deal to a few who come on it by chance or travel a long way to see it, than nothing to thousands. If that is excluding so be it. In future, if we are to protect and maintain, seclusion is sometimes going to be necessary and not only for Avebury. The sooner we accept this and act on it the more places we will be able to save.

About the author
PETER UNDERWOOD

Peter Underwood has been President of the Ghost Club (founded 1862) since 1960 and has probably heard more first-hand ghost stories than any man alive. A long-standing member of The Society for Psychical Research, Vice-president of the Unitarian Society for Psychical Studies, a member of The Folklore Society, The Dracula Society and a former member of the Research Committee of the Psychic Research Organisation, he has lectured, written and broadcast extensively. In 1987 he was elected a Fellow of the Royal Society of Arts. He took part in the first official investigation into a haunting; has sat with physical and mental mediums and conducted investigations at seances, been present at exorcisms, experiments at dowsing, precognition, clairvoyance, hypnotism, regression; conducted world-wide tests in telepathy and extra-sensory perception, and has personally investigated scores of haunted houses. Peter Underwood has written six titles for Bossiney – the most recent being 'Mysterious Places' and 'Ghosts of Dorset'.

Peter Underwood

Haunted Wiltshire
by Peter Underwood

The county of Wiltshire is famous for its prehistoric monuments. But it also has a number of interesting ecclesiastical ruins and buildings, castles and great houses that are full of splendour. And most of them are haunted.

Westwood Manor, near Trowbridge, is a treasure house dating from the fifteenth century and E G Lister, when he lived there, had no doubt about the place being haunted.

He talked to a Ghost Club investigator, Air Commodore Carter Jonas about the bedroom that was 'undoubtedly haunted' and of the several occasions when he had clearly seen the ghostly form of a woman in that particular room. As with many people who live in haunted houses, he took the apparitions and the sound of disembodied footsteps very much for granted and rarely discussed such happenings unless he was asked about them.

Much the same can be said of the present occupant Denys Sutton who tells me he believes there are now at least two ghosts in the house. He agrees that one bedroom is certainly haunted and although he often sleeps in this room he sometimes finds it 'distincty eerie' and on those occasions he sleeps badly. He has known several people who have no doubt about the room being haunted on intermittent occasions by some unidentified woman who seems restless. It would be interesting to discover who she is and why she walks.

Some years ago Denys Sutton told me he held a luncheon party at Westwood Manor when the guests included the then Danish Ambassador and his wife. When this lady was shown into the

Wiltshire, a haunted county overflowing with mystery.

'haunted bedroom' she immediately stopped short and said there was a ghost in the room. She had not known anything about the reputation the room has acquired over the years.

The other ghost at Westwood is a fearsome, silent, headless figure that wanders about the house. This strange, and also unidentified figure, was seen by Denys Sutton's predecessor and still occasionally manifests, especially in the presence of children.

*   *   *

Stourhead near Mere is a jewel of a place with magnificent gardens, temples and statues. The present house replaces a much earlier, haunted house and it seems that ghosts have remained at Stourhead and the surrounding area. The ghost of Charles, the Lord Stoughton, for example, haunts Kilmington Church to this day. And well he might, for it seems certain that the worthy Lord Stoughton, who was eventually hanged at Salisbury, engineered and probably took part in the violent and painful death of William and John Hartgill; notwithstanding the fact that they had systematically robbed the estate for years and had even destroyed the title deeds to the property.

Today the ghost of the doughty Lord Stoughton is sometimes seen on foot, sometimes mounted on horseback, making for Kilmington Church where the form disappears. In recent years some of the temples and statues at Stourhead have gained an unsavoury reputation, especially the impressive River God in his strange grotto with its walls encrusted with lava-like bricks. Several visitors have reported that they have been aware of some invisible presence there and others have told of odd experiences including half-glimpsed forms and shadowy figures haunting the vicinity. One photograph I saw seemed to depict a distinctly malevolent male form behind the River God on his right-hand side. It is an odd place and I have met a number of people who instinctively dislike the grotto for no apparent reason and who have heard voices and murmurings that have seemed to have no rational explanation.

*   *   *

Pythouse, the Georgian mansion near Tisbury, stands on the site of an Elizabethban house on land given to the Bennett family by the Abbess of Shaftesbury in 1225. The Bennetts owned the property until 1958. Some members of the family were distinctly eccentric, Colonel Jack Bennett for example, a hero of World War I, who was affectionately known by all and sundry as 'Mad Jack'. A complex character,

70

The ghost of the doughty Lord Stoughton is sometimes seen making for Kilmington Church.

generous one moment and mean the next, his unpredictable practical jokes were often puerile, sometimes cruel and usually just plain silly. His mother left Pythouse soon after her husband's death and never returned. She had never liked the house, any more it seems than she liked her only child, Jack, who says in his memoirs, 'I was always looked on by my parents as a bore'. She retired to her own property, haunted Preston Manor in Brighton, taking with her a great deal of Bennett silver, glass and china.

Jack was not mentioned in his mother's will; she left him nothing and Preston Manor was bequeathed to Brighton Corporation who turned the house into a museum and kept it much as it had been in the nineteenth century.

Early in the reign of Georve IV a tragedy occurred at Pythouse when Molly Peart, a nursery maid, had a child which she murdered at

71

The river god in Stourhead's grotto where strange voices and murmurings are heard.

birth. The identity of the father was never established although the butler of the day was strongly suspected. At all events Molly was sentenced to death and was in fact the last woman to be publicly hanged in England. Even as she died Molly threatened to haunt Pythouse, where she had been wronged, unless her remains rested there.

Her body was at first buried in a field, in unhallowed ground, but John Bennett, the master of Pythouse, aware of her dying threat, managed to have the body exhumed. The skeleton was articulated, placed in a coffin with a small glass window, and brought back to Pythouse and there placed in the cellars where it remained undisturbed for more than a century.

When Preston Manor became a museum, 'Mad Jack' decided they might like to have the remains of Molly Peart there. The skeleton was in a fine state of preservation and there was likely to be some interest in the remains of the last woman to be hanged in public . . . but as soon as Molly's remains left Pythouse, disaster struck.

At first only inexplicable sounds at night disturbed the inhabitants but the sounds grew louder and more frequent and a series of family misfortunes were blamed on Molly. Her remains were hurriedly and somewhat indecorously brought back to Pythouse and replaced in the cellars. When Pythouse was finally sold in 1958 to an organisation that was to become the Country Houses Association, Rear-Admiral Greathed, who founded the association, accepted that the skeleton of Molly Peart should never be taken away from the house, because dire consequences might result: Molly's threat to haunt the house was still taken very seriously. The mortal remains of Molly are to this day in the cellars and all is peace and quiet at Pythouse.

*　　　　*　　　　*

That respected author and explorer of historic houses, Allan Fea, did not have the fertile imagination so often evident in present-day writers on the paranormal. In common with his successor in the exploration of secret hiding places, my good friend Granville Squiers Fea was a member of the Ghost Club and as such exercised caution and brought a wealth of common-sense to his fascinating investigations. As one member put it, 'he recounts actual happenings, without any fantasy of the imagination.'

In the archives of the Ghost Club there is the account of one visit he made to haunted West Lavington Manor House with its room long reputed to be haunted by the ghost of Captain Henry Pewruddocke, a staunch Royalist who, during the Civil War, was shot by Cromwell's soldiers as he sat in an armchair.

In his signed report Fea says he had been shown the 'haunted room' by his hosts whom he had contacted for the purpose of researching one of his books and after a leisurely luncheon he was invited to explore the house as he wished. He says he spent the best part of a couple of hours poking about in various rooms until he arrived at the haunted chamber. Quietly opening the door he was

73

rather surprised to see the top of a man's head visible over the back of a chair facing the fireplace. Fea made sure there was some noise as he closed the door and when the figure made no movement, he decided that the man must be asleep. He was about to leave the room when something told him to wait. He stopped, just inside the door for several seconds, and when the figure still made no movement, Allan Fea quietly walked round until he was able to see the front of the chair and its occupant. What he saw was a man dressed in the showy clothes of a Royalist: a short jacket open to show the exquisite white shirt front and open on the arm through the slashed full sleeve; fine breeches ornamented with frivolous ribbon loops; stockings of silk and boots topped with lace. On the lap of the figure there was a brimmed hat with a feather in the side. The man did appear to be asleep and Fea, thinking he must have disturbed a member of the household whom he had not met, resting from some costume rehearsal, quickly turned to leave the room. When he had gone only a few steps he turned to make sure he had not disturbed the sleeping man – only to find the chair completely empty! As his hair began to rise at the back of his neck Fea quickly left the haunted room without a backward glance.

Fea adds in his report that he spent a night at Compton Chamberlayne, knowing that Henry Pewruddocke's kinsman John – who suffered for his part in the Wiltshire rising in 1655 – was said to haunt the old family seat. But there he slept peacefully and 'only made acquaintance with the Colonel's portrait and his night-cap.'

✳   ✳   ✳

The Marquess of Bath has been good enough to let me have details of some of the ghosts and legends associated with splendid and awe-inspiring Longleat. There have always been stories of Cardinal Wolsey riding in a coach on the night of the Crockerton Revels – in July – passing Foxholes and the Shearwater Bar Gate, and disappearing along the Horningsham Road but reliable reports are few and far between.

Longleat, home not only to the Thynne family but to many a spectre too.

Some remnants of a haunting may linger in a road called Five Ash Lane for it is a fact that many horses have refused to pass through Southleigh Wood at night. Time after time over the years, there have been reports of horses coming to a sudden halt for no apparent reason, and after standing stock still for a moment, they bolt back the way they have come – or attempt to do so.

Among many miscellaneous ghost tales there is the story of the Second Marquess who is said to walk the Sandwalk. 'James, the Watchman, declared he saw him', I am told. In the village there have long been stories of a 'lady in sheepskins' walking the top passages of the big house and Lord Bath believes this story stems from the actions of the Third Marchioness who, after her husband's death, was in the habit of taking her exercise there in a fur coat!

A local rector heard all about the 'lady in sheepskins' when he was a child and he always understood that some sort of exorcism had 'laid' a ghost at Longleat. He, and many others, were familiar with the legend of a Green Lady ghost: a passage on the top floor of Longleat has long been known as 'The Green Lady's Walk'.

The persistent story is that the ghost is that of Lady Louisa Carteret who married Viscount Weymouth, an unattractive man, by all accounts, both in appearance and in actions. Perhaps understandably Lady Louisa met and fell in love with a young man whom she managed to smuggle into Longleat. When they were discovered by her husband, a duel took place, fought up and down the top floor corridor, and it ended in the death of the lover who, according to legend, the Viscount had buried beneath flagstones in the cellar.

The corridor became known as 'The Green Lady's Walk' since the portrait in the house of the beautiful Louisa shows her dressed in green. And it is her ghost that is alleged to walk there, up and down, up and down, in an agony of grief. When central heating was installed at Longleat, centuries later, the remains of a young man were found under age-old flagstones in the cellar.

Then there is the ghost of Bishop Ken, reputed to return to his bedroom from time to time and always on the anniversary of his death – March 17 – when he sometimes reads his Greek Testament! This particular ghost and its activities became so troublesome that no servant would sleep in the affected room and it was turned into a china cupboard and lumber room.

The Red Library also has the reputation of being haunted and a number of people have reported the impression of some person or presence being in the room when the library is in fact empty. An elderly servant recalled that Lady Caroline, when she was a child, declared that she saw an old man in grey going through the door and, running after him, found the room empty. One of the house guides also saw a 'man in grey' in the same area and while the librarian Miss Dorothy Coates was working in the Red Library in the evenings – over a considerable period – she neither saw nor heard anything unusual but frequently had the distinct impression that someone was sitting beside the fireplace, a person who had either just spoken or was about to speak. Each time it happened, it was somewhat startling, for it was a very strong impression, although not really eerie or frightening; in a way it was in fact companionable, friendly even. Miss Coates thinks of the ghost haunting the Red Library as a 'nice, kind gentleman'. She just *knows* it is a man and that he is friendly.

On the other hand when the librarian had occasion to sleep in one of the bedrooms in 1948, where ghostly knocks had long been reported, knocks were indeed heard, practically every night. Sometimes the knocks were loud and at other times almost gentle. The sceptic might suggest expanding or contracting woodwork but the knocks were heard only once each night and always around the same time.

The immediate vicinity of Longleat seems to be very haunted. The ruins behind Woodhouse Farm have the ghost of a Cavalier who walks with his head under his arm according to local legend. The Lower Woods have long had the reputation of being haunted but by whom or what never seems to have been established. What is certain is that many people lose their way in the woods and come out distressed.

Among other legends at Longleat is that of a portion of a wall that projects onto the Longbridge Deverill to Crockerton road, some 50 yards north of the Longbridge Deverill churchyard. It is a wall known – for some undiscovered reason – as Dhu's Wall and there is a superstition that if ever this wall should fall, it will be the end of the Thynne family at Longleat.

During the First World War, the sixth Marquess' elder brother John, Viscount Weymouth, was killed at Hulluch in 1916. Oddly enough, before the news reached Longleat, but as it turned out, the day following her son's death, his mother and two of his sisters were driving past this portion of wall when they noticed several pieces of

A contemporary artist's impression of the Drummer of Tedworth producing his disturbances above John Mompesson's house from the Ghost Club Archives Collection.

stone had fallen from the wall. The Marchioness immediately ordered the pieces of stone to be replaced. To this day the wall is regularly inspected and kept tidy and in good repair.

*　　*　　*

Wiltshire was the scene of one of the most famous of all classic poltergeist infestations: the strange tale of the Drummer of Tedworth – now Tidworth. In 1661 or 1662 an itinerant drummer, William Drury, was apprehended to appear before John Mompesson, JP, who happened to be away. Drury's drum was confiscated, much to his annoyance, and at length it was taken to the Mompesson Manor House.

When John Mompesson returned home he was told that loud thumping and drumming noises had been heard all night by all the occupants and that night Mompesson himself heard the mysterious sounds. He searched for the cause of the sounds inside the house and then walked all round the property outside but found nothing to account for the noises which by this time had diminished to 'a hollow sound'. No sooner had he returned to his bed than the loud thumping and drumming noises recommenced, seeming to originate from the top of the house until eventually they 'went off into the air'.

The story is exceptionally well-documented and was investigated by the first real psychical researcher, the Rev Joseph Glanvil, who discovered that the sounds often centred around the bedsteads of the young Mompesson girls. The disturbances created considerable interest far and wide and the mysterious sounds and other happenings were witnessed by many visitors of standing and integrity. Eventually, some two years after they began, all the disturbances came to an end, as mysteriously and as as inexplicably as they started.

Wiltshire can boast of haunted stately homes, haunted cottages, haunted inns and haunted ruins; its ghosts are unusual and well-attested and they cry out for study, documentation and sympathetic investigation.

About the author
ALISON POOLE

Alison Poole is a Bristolian with her heart firmly rooted in the Westcountry. She was educated at Wycliffe School for Girls, Clevedon, and has childhook links and happy memories of Wiltshire. She remembers family picnics to Shearwater Lake near Longleat and tales of how father proposed to mother – who was stationed at Southern Command, Wilton, during the war – in the little summerhouse by the river in Wilton's municipal park.

She lives with her husband, a surveyor, their two daughters and a cat on Bodmin Moor. A well-known Westcountry journalist, she has lived in Cornwall since 1977.

A Scorpio subject, she is interested in history, archaeology – and tap dancing. In the autumn of 1988 Alison became Bossiney editor and she is currently writing 'Unknown Dorset', which will be published later this year.

Alison says she feels Wiltshire is a special county. 'Its stark uncompromising beauty inspires awe while its towns have a charm all of their own. It was in Wiltshire that I saw my first hare, sitting in the middle of a vast field' she said. 'And it was in Wiltshire too, not long ago, that I saw my first vicar on a bicycle!'

Alison Poole

Harvest of Mystery
by Alison Poole

IF extra-terrestrials really have been visiting this planet for a number of years it is hardly surprising they have homed in on Wiltshire as the ideal stopping off place. The county is literally bulging with manmade mysteries.

And if such wonders as Stonehenge, Avebury, Silbury Hill and the many ley lines which dissect the county are not just navigational aids then maybe there are other reasons which draw the space traveller.

Perhaps some galactical Cook's Tour entices the long-haul tourist to make that trip of a lifetime and pop down to England, a long standing favourite with visitors. 'Our tour starts at Wiltshire, a fascinating place just a short distance from England's main centre of population.' Whatever the reason there can be no denying the fact that Wiltshire, more than any other county, has clocked up a considerable amount of unexplained experiences.

The latest in a long line of strange happenings is the appearance of circles, usually in fields of corn. It does not sound so astonishing at first, but the frequency with which they have occurred over the last couple of years has already caused some ripples on official ponds – even central government is beginning to take notice, it is said.

Marlborough's high chalky downs in the top corner of the county have been the prime target for these mysterious overnight appearances, although Winchester, just over the border in Hampshire, seems to have a strong attraction too.

There was a flurry of activity in the summer of 1988 centred on the

Marlborough's high chalky downs look peaceful enough here but have been a prime target for mysterious happenings.

Tremendous energy has been detected flowing to the West Kennet Longbarrow from Silbury Hill seen in the distance.

Silbury Hill area. Silbury itself is an enigma, standing sentinel against the side of the main trunk road from Bath to London. Many theories have been put forward for its existence. Archaeological digs have been made, but nothing seems to satisfactorily unravel the riddle of this massive manmade lump of soil. Maybe its raison d'etre is something quite different. A force, a pull of such energy no man can begin to comprehend, just yet, what it is.

Brian Ashley of Avebury's Henge Shop has his own thoughts. Quite apart from being something of an acknowledged expert on the history of the area, Brian is also an accomplished dowser. He has detected tremendous energy through his dowsing particularly on the land opposite Silbury Hill. 'When dowsing there appears to be an energy tunnel where these circles appear' he said. 'The energy force goes from Silbury up to Longbarrow and flows south.'

In late July 1988, when the corn which grows so well in Wiltshire was just getting to a good height and ripe for harvesting, something seemed determined to have a little fun.

Overnight five mysterious circles appeared in a cornfield on land beside the A4 road at Silbury Hill, near Avebury. Just one week later another five appeared making a pattern of two large circles and eight smaller, satellite circles, all in the same field owned by the Hues family at Beckhampton.

Mr and Mrs Hues were justifiably puzzled, particularly as some of the circles were formed by the corn being flattened in an anti-clockwise direction while others were clockwise. The couple lost no time in getting on the 'phone to the RAF because helicopters from the Odiham base at Hampshire often carry out exercises in the area. But the RAF were adamant. It had nothing to do with them they said. And certainly it would have been nigh on impossible for aircraft to land at that spot because of the overhead power cables which run across it.

Freak winds or localised whirlwinds were proposed as a solution to the mystery. That idea found little credibility. If that were the cause the edges of the circles would have been ragged and irregular. They were neat and clean cut. Perhaps some lads were out for a lark. But in a field of corn marks would have remained where the pranksters had plodded through. There was nothing. A hoax was of course a reasonable explanation, but Mr Ashley, who was on the trail early the next morning, took pictures from Silbury Hill and he is quite sure there were no tracks whatsoever. 'The corn was not crushed, it was almost as if it had been layered' he said. 'There would almost certainly have been some evidence of tracks.'

A week later there were three more circles calmly sitting beside the others. That brought the total of circles which had appeared in Wiltshire that year to a staggering 54.

It did not stop there though. Only a fortnight later a Swindon private pilot spotted four small circles of flattened corn which were equally spaced around a larger circle, again close to Silbury Hill. He was rather taken aback by what he saw 500 feet below him as his single-engined light aircraft took a buffeting from air turbulence. In his 10 years flying he had never experienced anything like it before, although he could not be sure if the turbulence was related to the circles.

Colin Andrews is Technical Services Support Officer for Test Valley Council. He is also co-ordinator for the Circles Phenomenon Research Group. The circles, although prolific in Wiltshire, are not just confined to the county. The phenomenon occurs on a global scale. In fact, so great is interest in the circles phenomenon that some of the world's top scientists and engineers are devoting their energies to researching it.

The Circles Phenomenon Research Group is sure that a small number of circles have appeared from as early as the 1940s around the Salisbury area. 'And in fact,' said Mr Andrews 'there is evidence to support this.' He explained that there was a gap in data until 1966 when circles appeared in Queensland, Australia. Then in 1975 at Headbourne on the A34 near Winchester the first known recording ever was witnessed. Since then that particular site has seen a great proliferation of these circles. Along with Winchester, Warminster, too, sees these mysteries 'very, very, regularly.'

In the last three years there have been more sightings than ever before. In fact in four months in 1988 there were more than 100 sightings. 'Clearly we are looking at something new to us' said the man who is poised at the nerve centre of findings. 'Wiltshire, and Avebury in particular, is one of the most active sites in the world. If you put a compass on Avebury and scribe a circle enclosing a radius of two and a quarter miles, within that circle there will have been seen at least 28 formations in 1988 alone.' Mr Andrews believes many of the circles are the discharge pattern of a high energy field coming from within the earth or outside it. And this energy form is consistently on the increase right across southern England.

But it is not just England that is keeping an eye on developments. There have been increasing reports from Japan, Canada, America, Italy, France and a number of other countries where circles have been spotted. Along with the circles there have been other mysteries, such as amber coloured disc-shaped objects seen in the sky, things which are no strangers to Wiltshire either.

What can be causing the strange circular patterns in Wiltshire's cornfields?

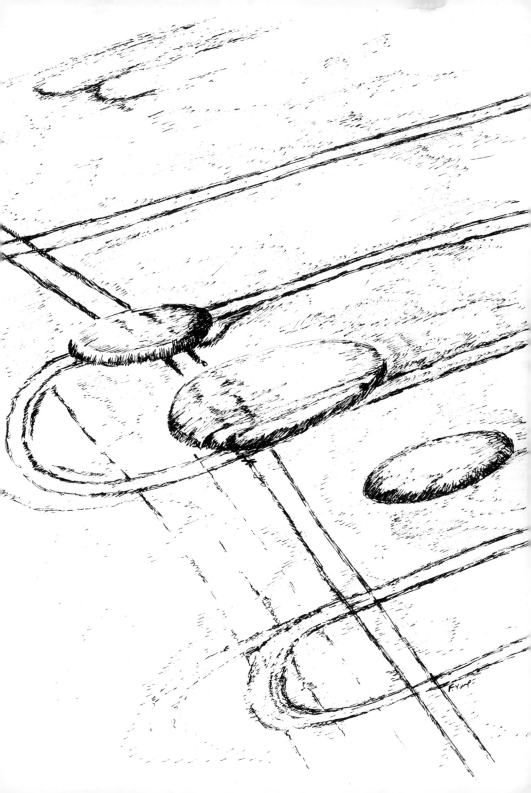

In Japan, there was a 25,000 gallon water loss from one paddy field where circles appeared, although there were no signs of a high element of heat to account for it.

The circles fall into three formation categories on the whole and within these they conform to fairly precise measurements. By far the most frequent pattern is the large circle, often to be seen in a cereal crop, which is compressed to the ground, and up to 30 feet in diameter. Then there are four smaller satellite circles which accompany it, each in the region of 13 to 20 feet in diameter, again with the crop swirled and compressed.

The phenomenon is not just confined to cereal crops. Across the world circles appear in all kinds of vegetation and some sites have even been spotted in snow in the Arctic or sometimes after a heavy hoar frost. Australia can boast circles in the sand but of course, with southern England a high cereal producing area, they are most frequently seen in fields of corn, rape or even grass.

Perhaps one of the most fascinating facets of this particular mystery is that there are strong links between the pattern and dimensions of these circles and those of the ancient archaeological sites such as Avebury and Stonehenge. Although these massive megalithic memorials to early man's superhuman efforts have excited awe, conjecture, hard-headed research and equally woolly-minded theories, nothing has ever been proved. Could they have been built in a specific place to take advantage of an area of force beneath the site? There is a suggestion that hidden water is the connection between these stone circles and mysterious underground forces.

The dimensions too are intriguing. Could there be a link between what is happening today, the circular impressions on the ground, and what happened 5,000 years ago when circular edifices were pain-

Silbury Hill keeps its silent vigil, refusing to give up the secrets of its existence.

stakingly hauled into position. Is there a common denominator? Did megalithic man have help from elsewhere?

Inextricably mixed with latter day studies of ancient sites in Wiltshire are ley lines. Leys were discovered by Herefordshire-born Alfred Watkins. He believed that these tracks, which follow an alignment of prehistoric points, were laid down long before Caesar's conquering army took Britain under Rome's protective arm. To Watkins ley lines were simply a way of prehistoric man getting from A to B before the days of county highway's network of signs and the wonders of the ordnance survey map.

Since his revelations in his book *The Old Straight Track,* which took the archaeological world by storm in the 1920s, his theories have found a massive following. And among these followers are those who believe that leys have a hidden field of force. Certainly leys criss-cross Wiltshire. Stonehenge and Avebury are sited on leys but Cley Hill, near Warminster, an enormous example of prehistoric architecture, seems to be the focal point for a large number of leys. And Warminster has long been acknowledged as a busy place when it comes to unidentified flying objects.

In the 1960s this delightful, quiet little town was projected into the headlines. Shimmering cigar-shaped lights, orange glowing balls of fire, noiseless silvery saucers, these and many more were spotted in the skies around the town, which until then had mostly been concerned with minding its own business.

Not all the UFO sightings were silent experiences. Sonic pressure waves, thunderous noises and even just whining and droning accompanied many Warminster residents' experiences. Tremendous gusts of wind were said to occur too. And whenever these things happened fear was left in their wake. Fear of the unknown. After all what could these strange lights be. When the Warminster manifestations were at their height in the mid '60s, as David Foot has explained, it was still some years before Neil Armstrong took 'one

Did megalithic man have outside help when these massive stones at Avebury were hauled into position?

92

small step for a man but a giant leap for mankind' as he became the first moonwalker.

A thick official blanket was dropped over the whole question. Military presence in Wiltshire, and particularly on Salisbury Plain is great. Most rational thinkers – who probably were not among those to have had a UFO experience – calmly blamed defence experiments or even bold espionage attempts from the Eastern Bloc. But still the tally of sightings gained in number.

After a hectic time in the '60s the UFO sightings tailed off – in Warminster at least. Life settled back into a more ordered pattern although occasionally something was still spotted in the night skies. And of course the memory lingered. It is a strange situation that a number of Wiltshiremen just seem to accept these unexplained visions. A very matter of fact young man was heard to comment 'I've often seen an orange ball-shaped light skimming across the sky and so have several people I know.' And another solid citizen of Avebury commented of the circle phenomenon 'People just seem to accept it. There is almost a conspiracy of silence much as there was in Nazi Germany.'

But while the ordinary folk of Wiltshire are left to puzzle, or just ignore, what is going on in their backyard, they can rest assured that mightier minds are carefully monitoring the situation.

The stark uncompromising beauty of Wiltshire with its smoothly rounded hills peppered with barrows and lone clumps of trees inspires awe. Even the light in the sky is different; sharp and unearthly. Little wonder then that this county alone has more mysteries to the mile than perhaps any other in Britain.

Marlborough Downs, a gentle rural scene which plays host to some strange manifestations.

Other Bossiney titles include . .

DORSET MYSTERIES
Bossiney invites six authors to probe mysterious facets of Dorset. The distinguished novelist Jean Stubbs, who sets the scene for *Dorset Mysteries* reflects 'This is a strange county, full of strange tales and superstitions.'

LEGENDS OF DORSET
by Polly Lloyd
The author explores legendary Dorset, visiting places as diverse as the Sacred Circle at Knowlton and Chesil Beach. Dorset is a mine of myth and folklore.
'Weird happenings . . . Polly Lloyd delves through tales ranging from moving rocks to murders . . .'
Ed Perkins, Southern Evening Echo

GHOSTS OF DORSET
by Peter Underwood
The President of the Ghost Club explores a whole range of Dorset hauntings. A ghostly white donkey, a world-famous screaming skull, phantom coach-and-horses story which Thomas Hardy used in *Tess of the D'Urbervilles* and a prehistoric 'Peeping Tom' are some of the subjects.
Ghost hunter Peter Underwood has been spook stalking in Dorset uncovering a host of eerie brushes with the Supernatural.'
Bournemouth Advertiser

MYSTERIOUS PLACES
by Peter Underwood
Visits locations that 'seem to have been touched by a magic hand'. The man who has been called Britain's No. 1 ghost hunter reflects: 'We live in a very mysterious world . . .'
'. . . an insight into some of the more mysterious places in the south west.'
David Elvidge, Launceston & Bude Gazette

SUPERNATURAL ADVENTURE
by Michael Williams
Contains a great deal of unpublished material relating to the Supernatural.
'Spiritual healing, automatic writing are just a few of the spectrum of subjects . . . neat, well-presented . . . easy-to-read volume.'
Psychic News

WESTCOUNTRY MYSTERIES
Introduced by Colin Wilson
A team of authors probes mysterious happenings in Somerset, Devon and Cornwall. Drawings and photographs all add to the mysterious content.
'A team of authors has joined forces to re-examine and probe various yarns from the puzzling to the tragic.'

UNKNOWN BRISTOL
by Rosemary Clinch
Introduced by David Foot, this is Bossiney's first Bristol title. 'Rosemary Clinch relishes looking round the corners and under the pavement stones ...'
'Not a normal guide ... it's a lovely book and very interesting ...'
Penny Downs, BBC Radio Bristol

SUPERNATURAL IN SOMERSET
by Rosemary Clinch
Atmospheres, healing, dowsing, fork-bending and strange encounters are only some of the subjects featured inside these pages. A book, destined to entertain and enlighten – one which will trigger discussion – certain to be applauded and attacked.
'... an illustrated study of strange encounters and extraordinary powers ...'
Somerset County Gazette

UNKNOWN SOMERSET
by Rosemary Clinch and Michael Williams
A journey across Somerset, visiting off-the-beaten-track places of interest. Many specially commissioned photographs by Julia Davey add to the spirit of adventure.
'Magical Somerset ... from ley lines to fork-bending; a journey into the unknown ... a guide which makes an Ordnance Survey map "an investment in adventure".'
Western Daily Press

100 YEARS IN SOMERSET
by Monica Wyatt
Spans the century in words and pictures.
'This is a lovely book. As you browse through the pages every picture seems to catch your eye and sends you off on a different track.'
Polly Lloyd, BBC Radio Bristol

PEOPLE & PLACES IN BRISTOL
Introduced by E. V. Thompson
Five authors take a look at People & Places in Bristol: E. V. Thompson, David Foot, Jillian Powell, Jack Russell and Rosemary Clinch.
'Words and pictures – many of them especially commissioned for this book – portray a rich Bristol heritage.'
West Review

MYSTERIES IN THE SOMERSET LANDSCAPE
by Sally Jones
Sally Jones, in her fourth Bossiney title, travels among the Mysteries in the Somerset Landscape. An intriguing journey among deep mysteries in a 'fascinating and varied landscape.'
'This is a whirlwind package holiday of sorcery and legend, touching down here and there before whizzing off in search of still more fascinating fare.'
Mid Somerset Series of Newspapers

E.V. THOMPSON'S WESTCOUNTRY

This is a memorable journey: combination of colour and black-and-white photography. Bristol to Land's End happen to be the Bossiney region, and this is precisely E.V. Thompson's Westcountry.

'Stunning photographs and fascinating facts make this a ideal book for South West tourists and residents alike – beautifully atmospheric colour shots make browsing through the pages a real delight.'

Jane Leigh, Express & Echo

DARTMOOR IN THE OLD DAYS

By James Mildren. 145 photographs.

James Mildren is an author who is at home in the wilderness of his Dartmoor.

'Lovers of Dartmoor will need no persuasion to obtain a copy. To anybody else, I suggest they give it a try. It may lead to a better understanding of why many people want Dartmoor to remain a wonderful wilderness.'

Keith Whitford, The Western

CASTLES OF DEVON

By James Mildren

James Mildren tours the castles of Devon: Castle Drogo, Lydford, Gidleigh, Okehampton, Dartmouth, Barnstaple and Watermouth are some of the castles featured.

'... a welcome addition to one's collection of Westcountry books. In all 17 castles throughout the county are looked at ...'

Elisabeth Stanbrook, The Dartmoor Magazine

HAWKER'S MORWENSTOW

by Michael Williams

A tour of North Cornwall immortalised by Robert Stephen Hawker who was vicar here for 41 years.

'... an insight into some of the more mysterious places in the south west.'

David Elvidge, Launceston & Bude Gazette

MYSTERIES IN THE DEVON LANDSCAPE

by Hilary Wreford & Michael Williams

Outstanding photographs and illuminating text about eerie aspects of Devon. Seen on TSW and Channel 4. Author interviews on DevonAir and BBC Radio Devon.

'... reveals that Devon has more than its share of legends and deep folklore.'

Derek Henderson, North Devon Journal Herald

We shall be pleased to send you our catalogue giving full details of our growing list of titles for Devon, Cornwall, Somerset and Dorset as well as forthcoming publications. If you have difficulty in obtaining our titles, write direct to Bossiney Books, Land's End, St Teath, Bodmin, Cornwall.